AF317021

# WORDS
# BREATHE
# 2

# WORDS BREATHE 2

## ROBIN TOTTEN

ISBN: Hardcover 979-8-3481-1791-7

Design and publishing assistance by The Happy Self-Publisher.

# DEDICATION

To my siblings Carolyn, Tracey, David, Kay and Kim

We didn't get to choose, but we make it work.

Life gives me words
Words make me write
Writing lets me breathe

For the gifts and callings of God are without repentance (Rom. 11:29).
Unearned, undeserved, freely given gifts. Our charge is to use them
for good, for the benefit of self and others. This is my use.

8

I come with instructions and some assembly is required. Please take the time to read the directions because the visuals may or may not be to scale.

# Let Me Reintroduce Myself

I rarely close doors. I don't close curtains at all. If you want to look, you should. I am fascinated by hummingbirds and natural springs. I ask that people own the lies they tell on me. I have never been fingerprinted. I am guilty of crimes that shall remain unnamed. I have broken every commandment save the sixth. I am at times hard-headed. I am not hard-hearted. My soul needs a continual weeding. I know a good gardener. I do not like soft fruits; my bananas and peaches have to be firm. I exhibit qualities that did not originate in me; they are modeled. My smile is genuine. So far, all my body parts are original. I sometimes retrieve things consigned to the trash pile. I recycle. I compost. I am not a runner. I cannot chase. I seldom know how much is too much. I clearly know when there is not enough. I abhor probationary periods.  I like little cars. I unapologetically, uncontrollably show compassion to babies and the elderly. I have become increasingly leery of two things. One is the obsession with space travel. We fail to steward well the ground we are on. Two is the abundant availability of seedless fruits. We may eventually be eating plastic. I am currently rethinking my 'no tea for the fever' type attitude. I do not intend to recline on hell's front porch. At times, my confidence offends. Though embarrassment may be the end result, I simply cannot check all the boxes.

At this age and this stage, I am learning, with regret, to leave people alone. It requires willful, deliberate thought.

# Missing Person

What is called proof is fallible; memory and sight do fail. Whether that happens suddenly or gradually, I do not know. Nevertheless, it was I who saw you last. Had I misplaced you? Put you in the wrong place in my environment.

Having a slight acquaintance with privacy, I won't vomit the curdled details that some request.

You may not want to be found, rescued, or gotten. Suffice to say, suspicion has befallen me. My motives now suspect. I am thus perturbed. But, back to you.

Yes, I can answer all the identity questions: full name, address, age, birthdate, height, hair color. All that and all that. Yada, yada.

Yes, of course, I know the details of when and where you were last seen. Yes, there are some unique physical characteristics. Again, this privacy thing though. Yes, your personal belongings are also missing. Yes, you have survival skills.

No, I cannot describe your clothing; what you were last wearing escapes me. Maybe it is nothing.

No, there is no law enforcement report. No, I will not agree to an interview. No, a reward is not being offered. We know what gets rewarded gets repeated. No, you did not leave a note or message. No, I did not contact your closest friend. That would require a meeting with me.

I am not indifferent to your departure; I just can't relinquish what was not mine. There is no crime in being missing. You voluntarily absented yourself. Proof that you ever were is fallible, making the notion that you could be found unsettling.

13

There are some lists kept only in my head. You're on that one.

# Nonfiction

There is no apprenticeship in life. You cannot work your way through from novice to expert.

Once upon a time, you came along and told your story. In the beginning, the back story:

Life was and is unpredictable, unexplainable, and difficult. Neglect, abandonment, routine. No interventions, no rescues. The extremes, from finances to food, and all Webster has in between, you knew too well. Too often. Honor and respect prepaid in advance to no avail. No one to trust. The slightest civil act masking an unrivaled disloyalty. Looks given that taunted. Actions taken that maimed. Words spoken that killed. The body, dead but not buried. Just hanging back, hiding like a shy child does. No teddy bears. No security blankets. Distress is your voice of comfort.

At the moment, living in contradiction. Not liking where you are due to hating how you got to this place. A personal failing. Though no one has asked you to, you keep the secrets.  A flaw. A mistake known in advance of making yet made. You are no good with straight lines. Thus, you scribble, you spiral. You vilify the wrong target. Distress is your choice of comfort. I'm afraid of fire. You bring fuel to my door. More practical than flowers, you say.

Everyone has a backstory. You think your story wretched. It is. Then, with monitored mouth, I speak.

15

Misery may love company, but it still has to be invited.

# Your Glory Set

Mine is truly an exercised imagination. However, the immensity of it all, too great for me. From the original beginning, stars sang. They never had to exchange trying for trust. They just are.

When night is put to sleep with bedtime whispers and in perfect sync, the alarm is sounded for dawn to rise and stretch out (snooze being foreign). The stars are not silent. The heavens declare.

When the vastness is wrapped in clear blue and refuses to preserve yesterday's clouds (no recycling), artistic newness every morning. The stars are not silent.

When the sun is commanded to stand guard the whole of the day to lavish the expanse in heat and light, its loyal reply is obedience. The stars are not silent. The skies proclaim.

From the fourth day, stars lived. Each one having a name. An intimate act of attentiveness; naming is. A knowing. This is not the thought of a mortal. For this they sing.  Stars are watching. They have their testimony (having a front row seat to it all). With no speech, stars sing. Science says their acoustic waves are too low for human ears. Stars sing, confirming the declaration that all of creation, everything, proclaim your glory. When stars sing, you are listening.

The archangel Michael sports an afro. His master has bronze feet and wooly hair texture. Not that God needs a color. Just saying. Hopefully, you will see for yourself.

# Silence

(Warning: this product contains harmful material. Someone was harmed in producing it.)

Just as I am getting used to company, becoming comfortable with being a comfort, I learn that there are emotions stored in hand grenades without pins scattered in random places. Some landing in my yard. Some at my table and in my bed. The language of the soul is emotion. And that is what held me longer than you did. Some have no soul.

No goodbye, see ya, farewell, out of here, au revoir, this isn't for me, adios, not interested, ta-ta, have a good life, later, ciao. No. None of these. Just silence. No language. Untold. Unknowing. Uncomfortable. Silence speaks volumes. Silence harms. Silence is a killer. It murders some. It butchers hope. It strangles desire. It smothers memories. It grows tentacles and attacks. It grounds bones to dust. When it became golden, I heard it clearly.

 A requested, required answer, replaced by silence, is cowardice. A quiet quit. I hear.  The reserved seat at my table, by personal invitation, could have, should have been declined.

All valuable things are vulnerable. Vulnerable things are subject to misuse. Misuse leads to abuse. Abuse is unacceptable.

20

# Soar

It is not dead voluntarily, but the messiness of life gives some earthbound worm the perpetual need to shut itself up in self-wrapped darkness. The shut-in is solitary. For even with the best of partners, a cocoon cannot be shared. Only later does it emerge transformed; what transforms comes from within. Brilliant, marvelous, wonderful, complex, and truly something else. Me too. A few trial flutters and I'm off.

I caution you not to memorize me. I'm changing. I contain contradictions.

22

# Night Ripped Off

Sunrise is a color not duplicated by Crayola or Sherwin Williams. It is an action not unlike a child having indulged in too many sweets. The sleepless night sky kisses the waking sun. A bursting erupts. Now energized, this fiery, fierce sun, for no other reason except it could not upstage the moon on the night before, crept spitefully through the spaces in the blinds. It splashed light at eyes that could close, hide, rest no longer. The blurry, thick veil covering a dream, hung vaguely in consciousness. Those irritating rays kidnapped the shadows of doubt, making the unwanted reality doubtlessly real. The truth exposed. Time to rise and shine. Dancing light gleaming about the room has successfully ripped off the last piece of night moon for me, a confined audience. Restless. Wakeful. Sleep deprived. I rise.

23

I've become proficient in absolutes that no longer serve me. The convictions I'm clothed in are sometimes debris, the perfume, acid.

# My Pandemic

There is a pandemic, and I am sick. With you.

At the onset, you impersonate an allergy. The right season anyway. I experience insignificant, minimal discomfort. A little itchy. I can breathe through it.

There is a pandemic, and I am sick. From you.

I've lost my sense of sight. You are transmitting infection. It's an imperfect time for masks. I need to see. I need to breathe. I have a fever, senses dull, body aches, pain. I've lost my sense. Rationality has picked my pockets and I am delusional.

"Are you Covid?" I ask. "No," you reply. "I am not." I had shot one and shot two. Had the boosters. I am sick anyway. The poison in my mouth tastes bitter. Exasperation. Agitation. Isolation. I've lost.

There is a pandemic, and I am sick. Of you.

It sounds minor now that the symptoms have subsided. Somewhat. So too you. Yes, you are Covid.

25

Medicine and poison are the same thing. Depending on the portion taken, you will get better or you will die.

# Best Life Ever
# (for Jamar)

It's almost Thanksgiving and I miss you. My nephew, the first to extend our family, making me an aunt.

Because your death is so hard to speak of and harder to believe, I cloak this truth in written form.

Thanksgiving is family time, and you, being a family man, loved that day. Me too. I fail to make sense of how it is that you're not here. Why you won't be present again.

Living your best life was impossible in the beginning. Circumstances beyond your control. You were a beautiful baby. A handsome boy. No matter. Your life was not easy. Not at two, at six, at twelve. You had a rough way. Surrounded by females. Estrogen filled ladies giving commands, making demands. Not one able to take on the full responsibility. Every one giving something. No one giving all. All with some level of control. All mothers, but not yours. You were given a home that you were never at home with. Their way; they did their best. No fault is found in them.

In due time, you tried your way. You failed and tried. Tried and failed. Never failing to try. You went a rough way. You learned that life is not fair. You wouldn't wallow in that though. No allowance for indulgence in self-pity. You chose power over pity. In that, you are your mother's child. You accepted the lot given. The ugly parts becoming your testimony. You came back. Fully transformed. Full grown, you would succeed. Living your best life became your motto.

You are among your own cloud of witnesses now. Reunited with your mother, grandmother, and great-grandmother.

One of them knows very little about you. Your mother disappointed her; she refused to recover. Reintroduce yourself. She's perfect now and so are you.

One of them knows the most intimate details about you. I believed she saved your life. Remind her of her valued family matriarchy.

One of them has been graced to see and know that in spite of all, you did well. Reconnect with her.

Days keep coming and going. I miss you. I am confident and comforted knowing you are now living your best life ever. Have a glorious Thanksgiving in heaven.  See you later.

Think of words and deeds as a loan that will be paid back with interest. The harvest, good or bad, is always greater than the seed. Always.

# Stormy

Thunder!  A tempestuous sound caused by lightning somewhere.

Lightning! An imbalance. The positive and the negative present and accounted for. Neither bow. Strong and rigid, scary and frigid. Who is it you think yourself to be? Hear the thunder. No darkness. No turbulence. No warning. Rapid discharge. Roaring and soaring and raging and staging.

Are you in the clouds or on the ground? Vice or virtue? Proper perspective is essential. The irony.

I hear your thunder. Like an angry fist banging on the door after hours. It echoes. Echoes and echoes. Just sound; noise really. Loudness. No rain. No reign. The exclamation point morphed into a question mark. That lightning, now that's remarkable. It is mighty, potent.

Black sheep, because of their relatively coarse wool that cannot be dyed, are seldom used in garments. Lucky them.

# Merger

A takeover of the non-hostile type. You assume control of and responsibility for the acquisition.

You had me at "Do you want anything?"

For you knew I had come to need nothing. Not your time (though restricted). Not your talent (though astounding). Not your resources (though liberal). I found it imperative that the zone of comfort offered be an improvement to my solitude. An upgrade.

You had me at "Do you want anything?"

Want is different. Want is action. Want is limitless. Want is yen.

Want is edgy yearning, with borders touching envy. Want wears oversized jeans, pockets filled with appetite and craving.

You had me at "Do you want anything?"

I don't usually take what is offered. For my legs won't carry me where my mind travels. How do I begin to answer this loaded question?

Yes. No. Sometimes. Maybe. Want invites assumptions. Some faulty, some not so much. Want is an inconvenient subgroup of need. Solitude is good. We went for great.

All this queen's wit with all this queen's zen could barely fuse reason together again.

You had me at "Do you want anything?" Nothing taken away. Nothing left behind. No imagination needed.

"Ooh child, things are going to get easier." Jurisdiction granted. Takeover.

Romance is an idle idol, useful for little to nothing.

# Take Him Leave Him

For all the little people who have touched my love
and my life. Know, He (God), is with you everywhere.

I would, I could, take Him, leave Him there. And still, He's with me everywhere.

In the dark, for a bad dream. At the park, when friends are mean.

At the doctor's, or when there's pain. In my house, when I'm to blame.

In the classroom, when I don't know. At my game, when the score is low.

I could take Him, leave Him there. And still, He's with me everywhere.

When my choices are not that good. When I don't behave like I should.

When loved ones die, it's sad; so true. Others feel bad, all around you.

I would take Him, leave Him there. And still, He's with me everywhere.

When I get mad and you get mad, and mad is how we want to be.

When bullies come and knock me down. When friends are there but make no sound. I could take Him, leave Him there. And still, He's with me everywhere. When big world problems touch my heart with things little hands had no part. I wonder. Will I grow up living good? I hope I do. I think I should. On days when I say, "It's not fair." All you say is "I don't care." When hope of having fun and such is lost because things cost too much. The times the day monster comes to hurt and kill. Not hiding, not pretending. This one is real. I would take Him, leave Him there. And still, He's with me everywhere. When I'm afraid cause you're afraid. Life gets too hard and I'm too shy. I'm not a baby, but I do cry. I really like to keep Him near. I really have to have Him here. And if you need Him, He is there. He is with you everywhere. You can have Him. This is how. Tell Him that you need Him now.

I can never forget whom I have touched, whom I have loved, long after I don't want to remember. Memory betrayal.

37

# Overture
# (With Intentional Order)

Overall, overjoy overdrive overdose oversight overactive overboard overachieve overstock overcompensate overextend overflow oversee overtime overdrawn.

Overall, overcast overexposed overlook overlay overlap overnight overreact overstate overpower overstep overshadow override overkill.

Overall, overbearing overload overrule overturn overcome overdue, over you.

Though ignorance is bliss, it is also expensive. I have the receipts.

# Tin Man

Woodchopper, where is your heart? Remember from whence you came. Emotional. Compassionate. Brave. With your signature ax causing bodily harm, you chopped, one by one, your own limbs. Nothing remained. Love costs an arm and a leg literally. Tin Man, faults are excusable. Inexcusable are the strategies employed to hide them. The urge, the need to default always, to insouciance. Dusty. Rust is the anesthesia chosen to deaden feeling. Rusty. Top to bottom, eye to ass, rust and dust. Who will oil you? Unlike plastic forks from a favorite takeout, hearts are not disposable.  Hearts are not for sale. Buying one is not an option. Therapies and self-care will not exchange for one. Hearts are grown. With the oil of compassion, a stretch of empathy, the massage of goodness, hearts are constructed.  This is not Oz. The outer covering, be it silk, cashmere, or velvet, cannot conceal the sawdust. A real heart is a requirement.

40

It has been discovered that sometimes, comfort and convenience borrow love's clothing (and dress to impress).